Spectra

Spectra

ASHLEY TOLIVER

COFFEE HOUSE PRESS
Minneapolis
2018

Coffee House Press books are available to the trade through our primary distributor, Consortium Book Sales & Distribution, cbsd .com or (800) 283-3572. For personal orders, catalogs, or other information, write to info@coffeehousepress.org.

Coffee House Press is a nonprofit literary publishing house. Support from private foundations, corporate giving programs, government programs, and generous individuals helps make the publication of our books possible. We gratefully acknowledge their support in detail in the back of this book.

LIBRARY OF CONGRESS CATALOGING-IN-PUBLICATION DATA

Names: Toliver, Ashley, author.
Title: Spectra / Ashley Toliver.
Description: Minneapolis : Coffee House Press, 2018.
Identifiers: LCCN 2018004535 | ISBN 9781566895262 (softcover)
Classification: LCC PS3620.O3283 A6 2018 | DDC 811/.6—dc23
LC record available at https://lccn.loc.gov/2018004535

PRINTED IN THE UNITED STATES OF AMERICA

25 24 23 22 21 20 19 18   1 2 3 4 5 6 7 8

For Joseph

Spectra

KINESIS

Though all bird-legged creatures fear
the same distance, it is instinct that pulls
them to standing. In the museum
their bodies like sea glass, an astonishment.
The specialist says we can classify species
by measuring height with our hands:
All but the smallest flamingos must stand
eight palm-lengths from the earth.
Their legs are the width of paper clips.

This kind of gauging is necessary. To a child,
the globe is cross-hatched dark blue, and it is.
Mathematics form a tent frame. In this way,
a sunrise is one kind of blood, oxidizing.

Today I read in the *New York Times* that Africa
is splitting in two. Land is metastasizing,
spilling open, and sinking. Ethiopia is covered
in holes. I say I am speaking in present tense
but all scientists say we are watching
an ocean, growing at staggering speeds.
Can we say this is a continent, *oceaning.*
Once, I heard a father tell his older daughter,
you are a clear pool where light plays. Though she
had also been an island orbiting a large body.

Is this a natural disaster

The thing we feared most in the fires was logic:
We watched the flames leap from the field
to the trees to the house in succession.
Though we found it familiar, close
in its grammar, most of us stayed inside.
Today Oakland firefighters are made out of paper.
They write birch-soaked memoirs. They have
lungs like parachutes and spit up sap oil.

Our urgency comes because
we too are upright, a vertical people.
We are possessed by margins.

I am thinking of the mother who drowned
her three boys, why she stopped first
to undress them. If she was perfecting
a displacement of water, plumbing a violent
kinesis. It was late, on the pier, where one witness
remembered: *I saw a woman sitting on a bench
gazing at the water, occasionally looking
from side to side as if she was waiting
for someone.*

I.
HOUSEKEEPING

KING

At night I am Egyptian, and you
are the last pharaoh. When the battle is

over, I drag your body through cool
blue water. Your blood is diesel

on the surface, the birds dive in and out.
At the end of your arms the battering rams

are quiet. Underwater they dream
fence dreams, dream splintered wood.

The continent is still but all the shades
of gold remember you: poppy, stone,

stars and arches, certain roots and windows,
the whole earth in an early stretch of dusk,

mirror, fire   they shake, they shake.

HOUSEKEEPING

Under enormous strictures the salt hinges, becomes a fold. Underneath the canopy I dressed in white like stitches were anathema to waking. A hush at the collar makes binding notes. You smear the water. Past the pointed periphery, out past the lake notes miming the subject, I stand up straight like a clasp on the light boards, catching favor. In the daytime, nothing lingers. Pull all the maps inside.

HOUSEKEEPING

A move shaking west in suburban fleet, you pen martyr versions of our softest reasoning. Downtown haze of what we skipped over, flint and a scratch on the lens, street bulb. Making a mess of things. Outside, the sodium lamps refuse even a glimmer. Thrush lies under the surface. Awake again during cemetery hours I hunt for our vows in all the outspoken positions. You never get to the point.

HOUSEKEEPING

Inside your latest vision of matrimony, we meander in taller shoots and rails. Static underling, I come clad in my birthday shoes for letting the ancestors sleep. The music comes through or it won't, though you listen in harvest proportions. Grey gaze at the museum wall, light fractures in frame. It's only a small turn: you posture by degrees.

HOUSEKEEPING

A pocketed wailing beneath clean clothes is what. Making hair
pulled taut into windows just the same. At the end of my rope
is something shaped like tipped sails, the water rushing clean
over the hull. There's something we've left behind, but not in
the way you'd think. It's how the metal works, cut in emerald
poses. We stand to let the green in.

HOUSEKEEPING

Dear night possessor: your funeral barge rocked tight in the fisting water makes small winter melodies. The light ends a pattern we learned to stupefy by motion or admitting away. A statutory list puts the blame on the hour. You move as I move, whistling measures in salt grass, patient and guarded processions. At night, the line is a current to wade through: older names sifting past the flotsam, the water rising up to here.

LONG DIVISION

carry the husband
given to speech
show us how light
can be flayed in-
to the last of something

nightshade and vegetal
he stands in the river

half-Deschutes, half-
man listening
for a woman

to crawl out of
herself—

HOUSEKEEPING

Away from the glow, a dumb bulb freezes in its wintery malaise, covering the rest of the light. I don slippers and wait for the impact in all the right places: a notebook and photograph, a letter you once wrote. Of course we can climb backward into the pulp and pull all the questions from their sharpened hangers. I'm doing it already, see me, I'm pulling all the shredded lace down, quitting in the middle of the song.

HOUSEKEEPING

A tick of blonde beaming wide, or return to a messier proof.
You stymied in the river there just there just the same. No one
comes measuring the granite. No one comes wading in. The
sky is a rip in the seawall cut in two, hairline indisposed in
sleep. I can almost see Manhattan from here, where we raise our
matchsticks like cutlery, where we are singeing our most decent
parts. Inside an ordinary room our bodies flatten and spread
over the furniture like breakers catching the last of the sun.

HOUSEKEEPING

At night I stand at rapt attention slamming the kettle water back.
I thought planning commensurate with purposely fraying an
architecture you entered by looking. Swell and a ghost between,
like some perfected anchor leached into the drinking water:
crease in the filigree, mild grace in execution.

HOUSEKEEPING

Dear stone fruit: I haven't wept anywhere in at least seven days. Outside the lunar engine clicks and flinches. I go on gargling with port wine, heavy dashes of clipped lullaby. Dear stone fruit: today's is a season for waking to ankle weights roused from our darkest houses. The light angles over the net in a drastic lunge to pivot. Point. Counterpoint. All that we came for irradiates.

HOUSEKEEPING

Under implied direction the lace steps to honeycomb, turns pictures. From a long-legged point of view, the line finds an edge to root against. I haven't left the house in fifteen days and still like a surface decoration poised in front of the window I stand for whoever comes snapping the shutters. To hear you speak is one of the finer prisms hugging the knife-board in secret. Oh how I wind down like real wool at the hinges, give off the most natural pill. Light catches a peak on the fold and you hung there, strung like a lifting bell.

THE LOOMSTRESS LOSES HER LINEAGE

no wilderness body catapulting the staircases
kissing the hemlines of her
one mark of reach   she sits down

no wait anymore   no passive geometry
she   a loom hung quiet now

listen to him   hull avocados in the kitchen
maybe she like a fruit skin peeling back
from the hearth, peeling back from the dining room table—

but she is one come unlined   no pocketed weight
womb in a peach-fist borne bare on the branch

no rub of knuckles mimicking hers
no molar membranes greening

(how to gut a fish in your absence now)

will he stretch the bit   urchin husband
when she is a bridge receding the river

will he wade out of the bedroom now   refusing

when the minute folds over and she stands
outside it   a snap in the violin neck

HOUSEKEEPING

A burr on the inner sleeve of expecting miracles, I stand to take down the hooks. Where a rise should set in, nothing takes. Say I dry heave at luxury, placating asphalt for rarer tricks of the light. Blame where the invisible goes.

HOUSEKEEPING

Beyond the last bridge to the subject you pull to replace the draw-line, a hardened taste in the mouth. At least one happiness in the dozen dries out. For any chance of lightning indoors, ring the room in elaborate glass. Neck-deep in your broken-bell stature a grin rips out to cross the chalk.

HOUSEKEEPING

Tepid blow cools the liquid to hunch and wind. A box arrives and loaded spills order across the floor. Living room, dining room, room of tinder and kindling. The joints grind to aspirin under the whitest application. At night I place oil over all the door hooks to make for swifter leaving. Kerosene opening, I saw it coming and took flight.

STANDING ON THE LAWN OUTSIDE YOUR HOUSE WITH A MATCH AND A GALLON OF GASOLINE

This morning in the cupboard I found
your last quarter inch of whiskey settled amber
in the mason jar same burn on the horizon
the last Indian summer you sat naked
at the kitchen table carving the nectarines
free from their stones

When the cold math of winter arrived early
that year I thought the first fist you seamed
into my cheekbone was to get to the proof,
to the pit of the marriage

You asked *if somewhere we find the itch
of the lumber do we find compassion
for the ax blade that splits it—*

I used to lie down inside my own stitches
and let the dawn-light farm their black
to noon, now I run like a ragged dog over
the tight bow of their edges: it doesn't make
any difference what angle I work
my heart against them,

I still don't know what kind of woman
I am. But as the flame nears the fingers
that trust the match, as close as the skin
can stand it to singe, I call this the nerve
to find out—

II.
IDEAL MACHINE

dear daughter   *you lived—*

here is where I take you   behind the eyes
a glistening star

here is where I take you

                  bone-thing I made
                      a gift
pull it out

        star in me   salt bright and still

                        listen
how the cut is made
        across my face could move any feeling

here is the site I've dog-eared for you

        taut as any waiting
my sudden fold of luck

                pinched lightning
we can't put our hands on but   you do

my brain arriving through the darkness
        like streets mapping out

this mine   this mine   this mine

in future rites   I lie down
                              on the operating table

glassy and overdue
the surgeons   take roll in choirs

hands like night swimmers
                              badwater below the sea

under lightest implication
          the body breaks through

under lightest implication

the crocuses push
                    through peat as a gesture for belief

hourglass and tulle
meadow sharpened to blade

                    on the last day the light
                              so easy to breathe

hustle star
               weaving the darkness around

a little let on the line   and
faces go under

                              a long way

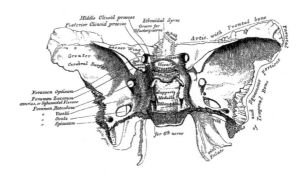

fig. 1

dear Lepidoptera

I can't stop saying
your name

dear optic nerve
you flatten like copper tilled wide
                              against the tracks

I want to show you how light scatters
my daughter's bedroom   her face
                              into unknowing

dear optic nerve   dear crushed penny

in the dark I watch explosions
                    axons firing like mortars
                              I count them

low-hanging fireworks
                              gristle and verve

I press my face to the glass

I slim to wrench   my one good eye
over the room like a loaded drink

everything whirs into focus   then out
                                     the air
and my face behind it
          unwinding the gauze
                         scrim on the scene

we could spend years like this

just you and I together
in the same crowded bar

spinning our whiskey for weeks before
knocking them back   one by one

the lamplight growing vague   then dim

where is your face
I say to the dark
                        look

everything is turning
into everything else

moth shuttled inside   an empty glass
paper slid over the mouth

dear ophthalmologist
your hands wag the story I cleave to

                                on either side of my face
wave fingers   ask me to count them

dear ophthalmologist
     I am not very good at telling stories

how your hands muscle the black

                        pinpricks in the paper
how the dark   whistles around them

day   a dumb animal
                  limping through the grass

from the observation wing   we can see it
            gathering size

slow and sensate
I enter the machine   like a lover's black silk

my astronomer
flipping on all the lights

    meat of the mind   wrung to transparent

he points to where the shine
                 breaks open from seed
      hustle star

                   star in me

the bone   first   anatomical   then moth
        then

               Lepidoptera

O don't we all saunter in
innocently enough
        like love   an uppercase *L* love

stamen eye   you metastasize

          my sea glass   my meteor

fig. 2

dear Lepidoptera
here is the root   *let them cut you*

close your eyes   what do you see

a pocketknife placed   in the hands of a girl
who turns over
the first matter:
                    what can I make   *a boy*

                    begin here

here   where the wood brightens
between her fingers
the gate of the mind's redress

                                        with the body
she coaxes to peel from itself like magic

the intent to un-suture   layer after layer
                                        raking free

vulgar eye waxed   blind to wonder

in the morning I drag the crane fly   dead
across the mirror   seeping
                              I gather what's left
legs curled to pills
one after another

                         in this universe
several species of matter
                                    destroy matter
in long conversation
                 mosses unbraid the trees
                                    from themselves

earth into air into space
where something else was

we are never   not alone
we are never not   alone

outside the window
                              a line curves to curl to
kite string caught in the cypress
one end whorled to nest

there is light   in us yet:

        everywhere we look   tassels unravel
into brighter and brighter knots

these are the days   outside of all days

my earth wheeling toward you
teeming with self   split   into jewels

relentless figures   I hoarded
                      so patiently—

   who brought you here   shadow
            behind my eyes
to blot out the distinctions between things—

ellipsoidal planets   tethered by blood
my little   mussitation
           it was my
                  didn't know

the fetus consumes the mother   the tumor
consumes the mind

dear son   I harvested you from this

as any winter   saws the youngest
spruce on the plain

silencer placed on the note
                and hummed there

repressive gesture frozen around
the snuffed-out kin

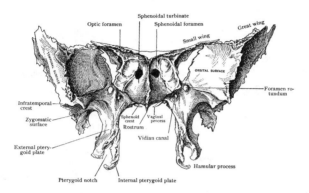

Optic foramen · Sphenoidal turbinate · Sphenoidal foramen · Small wing · Great wing · ORBITAL SURFACE · Foramen rotundum · Infratemporal crest · Zygomatic surface · Sphenoid crest · Vaginal process · Rostrum · Vidian canal · External pterygoid plate · Hamular process · Pterygoid notch · Internal pterygoid plate

fig. 3

dear Lepidoptera

womb of the mind

inside you our son splays to life

a lover is always on his way   into the room
inside the mind

he wants to break the glass
casing on the firm grace-thump

                                        from the bulb

we wait for him
                    we wait for him

he wants to cut   where the cells have listed
                                        something to do
with his hands

                                        he wants to find
where what is burnished is buried

where the air snatches the light to hum against

            the light   like a grass-blade   tucked
between the thumbs

                lunettes of dark   against
the bone

he wants to catch me   between his thumbs

the body strung with ornaments   they
            cannot fly   they
can only stand still

                    we walk the little
halls of my body   pale stepping-stones
        jarred mercury

dear surgeon   let's say
we try it: put my tongue to curette
let you   carve in

                at night
the room fills with children   each one
of them ours   they flame around
in their gene pools

live instruments   tuned   shivering
the glass
                a little resonance

picture-postcard   hair behind the ear
just the same   place is a curl
you can touch it

the intersection a line
                        drawing back to intervene

tissue and bone   a moan one makes
the hand that lifts
to clavicle   one note pulled to crater

they can sing or forget

                                to sing

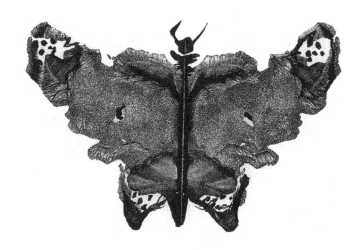

fig. 4

dear daughter   *you lived*

dear daughter   you lived:

born before the clean sweep
twinning above you

                      halo   moot lightning

handful of grey carnations   you appeared
analogous in frame

                         a stitch of beyond-me
dull pearls   you began to speak by blossoming

dear daughter
                in an instant I become cinematic

my trigger finger
gives silk to the knot and he grows

        hustle star

                                star in me

dear son   don't flinch
when he comes for you

        singing through my brain   my face

lure   you wait
shadows flat under the operating lights

                              scissor to flower to bone

walking downhill   with her brother
the noon sky reversing   to ink

storm of stem cells and blue-black blood
                                    they exhale
through twin sets of lungs

slowing   her brother   sits her down
  on the curb
                      lifts a nickel to his sternum
to turn open the lock: *here is the stone*
I've been polishing for you

he places the bullet in her palm
like flotsam

my sea glass   *my meteor*

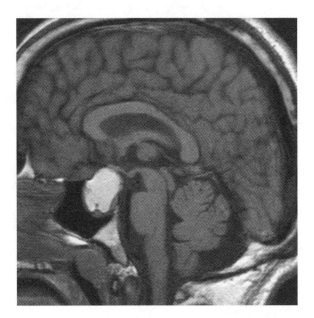

fig. 5

if it is a crown   *it must belong*
to a king   or a bloom   *in shallow water*
nine months less likely   *to be patiently touched*

surgeon I wanted   to love you
                 corrected
pulley   screw   lever   torque

I wanted to lie   just there   underneath you

            patient
                         silent as space

from the window the bridge spans clean
over the water

               the most elegant way
                   to cross the river

the most elegant way   to split
                   the face

I wanted to show you
how decent it is   to make something small
               so   easy to find

outside the body   you cue the instruments

I brace and practice   lifting my weight
through gaps in belonging

         the most elegant way
           to cross the river

            the most elegant way
               to split the face

you open the woman   I was
     like a flask

you said *just for me*   you said *no going back*

a coiled thing   slipped pattern
in aperture

filiform blade turning   my magician   pulls
from the skull an animal   first humming
                    then flaming

heavy hive with the wrong birds inside

people fall in
                and out of love all the time

at night I place our son   between my teeth
tender roe   bones
            brittle as mica

see how the mother-parts shine
the amber lake I am building around them

tiny whirl   blister of
                            architecture   cold music

blood is the first color I spin

                        my desire around

and clasp behind my neck

snarled in my translucency pose

I kneel at the face   black-thread inseams

                        a place you can cross

I wanted to see   an indelible edge

    a line   lit   inside the mind—

your hands inside me   then   lemon

brain cells   glittering like night geodes

reeling and numinous—

instead I lie   whole brain yawning out

stretched against the blue

                      to ride out to

dear reader   I slept

fused to him a dull

                sleep of him

blinking on again   and off like a strobe

                      my magician

at the foot of my bed like a scalding vicar

foamed   my face is a yolk that spreads

                    across air

    rush of cells

coiled memory

                wonder

        it leaks from us

        everywhere

dear tiny icicle   you barely existed   though
                                                 enough

you were not meant to be mine
you were not meant to be made

I lean out   over the bridge
                              let you fall and burst

I place the nickel   in your mewling mouth
don't remove it

on days when I'm feeling   especially cold
I ride through my own

                  icebox of logic

once I chose   life over death

               how mundane

death is the last   road to awe I know

III.
SPECTRA

here is the first thing   in the second earth:

mimosa blossoms
radial mimetic of energy   stamened into sky

cerulean singing against the clean
                                        white buds

                  across the strawberry fields
          thaw   and what survives

                                the breaking into
                                        heat   given freely

to outrun the cantering dark

                          ***

there is no northern limit
                    to the capacity   for awe:

leaving the sea   a child
                                        throws the light
                          back at the sky like a chucked blade

waves on the winter water break into
careful pleats

there is a vigilance to it   the desire
                                to include everything

tulips pouring out
of the lean earth

atlantean fists   bulbs   big as brains

                          ***

why is the dark
so dazzling   abacus
                    as much net   as mirror

dear slow-motion enemy
soft as milk

we can make an eden   out of even this:

larvae swimming
                            in the black earth
absorbed and absorbing the universe
      the apples fallen   ripe
through the sheer breeze—

            the totality will catch you
            the totality will let you go—

turned glossy as diamonds

        wet   with their own certain aliveness

                            ***

I want to sit with you
in the molten-
hot center of things

                hunger and silence
                entirely minted

                    we only have so much time

        held   still
the breath is the breadth
that outlines the whole

this phenomenal body
great machine of a body
                              that turns
                        as a blossom turns

somersaults of fragrance and rot

                  I close
my eyes and see
how the wind hulled the valley
                                    honestly

despite itself

            ripening
magic on top of
  magic on top of
                        magic

                  ***

there is a way to the light   if we want it:
familial fingerprints   gold-
                  threaded globes
                  on the windowpanes

and beyond them   an allegiance that fans out

      beyond the buoys
                              beyond the bridge lit
                              inside the mind

out of the only   country we know

out where the darkness is a mirror   seen
through to
                              the place beyond
                              dimension

beyond the last blue rift in possibility
where everything splits   and shimmers

beyond what brought us here
and what will take us back

                         ***

it is dusk   on earth   I see
                              myself through you

in the last pew
                  of the lit horizon
in the wide-open field of the now

the gaze is the fabric
                        that wraps the whole world

across the blue tilt   salt lick
the only country we know
blinking with warmth
                                    and a belonging
                  that grows   as a tulip grows

plunged into darkness   then
                              emergent

neon unraveling toward the next   kind thing

                         ***

INDEX OF FIGURES

ACKNOWLEDGMENTS

Many thanks to the editors of the following publications in which some of these poems first appeared: *Copper Nickel, Design Observer, Front Porch Journal, PEN America, Third Coast, Redivider,* and *Sonora Review.* A number of the poems from "Ideal Machine" appeared in a chapbook of the same name published by Poor Claudia.

I am so grateful to the many who were part of bringing this book into the world: Adam Plunkett, Hafizah Geter, Ama Codjoe, Caitlin Dwyer Young, Ruth Ellen Kocher, Monica Bahan, Stacey Tran, Jonterri Gadson, Robin Coste Lewis, Tameka Cage Conley, F. Douglas Brown, Zachary Schomburg, Drew Scott Swenhaugen, Donald Dunbar, Amie Zimmerman, Kyle Buckley, Ezekiel Pfeifer, Liz Mehl, Justin Rigamonti, April Coppini, and Samantha Wall.

My deepest gratitude also extends to the institutions and collectives who granted me the time, space, support, and funding to help me complete these poems: the Academy of American Poets, Brown University, the Cave Canem Foundation, Oregon Literary Arts, Poetry Press Week, Pomona College, and the Taxidermy Salon.

Thank you to my editor, Erika Stevens, and to the entire CHP team for their unremitting patience, insight, and instinct.

Special thanks to my family: to Joseph Mains, for his steady hand and enormous heart; to Djuna, Ovid, and Onnavah Mains, for their light and perspective; and to my parents, Jackie and Pat Morrisey, for their love and celebration.

This book wouldn't have been possible without my teachers: Claudia Rankine, C. D. Wright, Forrest Gander, Cornelius Eady, Michael S. Harper, Paul Mann, Renee Gladman, Cole Swensen, Toi Derricotte, Terrance Hayes, Carl Phillips, and Allison Benis White.

These poems are dedicated in memory of C. D. Wright and Michael S. Harper.

LITERATURE
is not the same thing as
PUBLISHING

Coffee House Press began as a small letterpress operation in 1972 and has grown into an internationally renowned nonprofit publisher of literary fiction, essay, poetry, and other work that doesn't fit neatly into genre categories.

Coffee House is both a publisher and an arts organization. Through our *Books in Action* program and publications, we've become interdisciplinary collaborators and incubators for new work and audience experiences. Our vision for the future is one where a publisher is a catalyst and connector.

FUNDER ACKNOWLEDGMENTS

Coffee House Press is an internationally renowned independent book publisher and arts nonprofit based in Minneapolis, MN; through its literary publications and *Books in Action* program, Coffee House acts as a catalyst and connector—between authors and readers, ideas and resources, creativity and community, inspiration and action.

Coffee House Press books are made possible through the generous support of grants and donations from corporations, state and federal grant programs, family foundations, and the many individuals who believe in the transformational power of literature. This activity is made possible by the voters of Minnesota through a Minnesota State Arts Board Operating Support grant, thanks to the legislative appropriation from the arts and cultural heritage fund. Coffee House also receives major operating support from the Amazon Literary Partnership, the Jerome Foundation, McKnight Foundation, Target Foundation, and the National Endowment for the Arts (NEA). To find out more about how NEA grants impact individuals and communities, visit www.arts.gov.

Coffee House Press receives additional support from the Elmer L. & Eleanor J. Andersen Foundation; the David & Mary Anderson Family Foundation; Bookmobile; the Buuck Family Foundation; Fredrikson & Byron, P.A.; Dorsey & Whitney LLP; the Fringe Foundation; Kenneth Koch Literary Estate; the Knight Foundation; the Matching Grant Program Fund of the Minneapolis Foundation; Mr. Pancks' Fund in memory of Graham Kimpton; the Schwab Charitable Fund; Schwegman, Lundberg & Woessner, P.A.; the U.S. Bank Foundation; and VSA Minnesota for the Metropolitan Regional Arts Council.

THE PUBLISHER'S CIRCLE OF
COFFEE HOUSE PRESS

Publisher's Circle members make significant contributions to Coffee House Press's annual giving campaign. Understanding that a strong financial base is necessary for the press to meet the challenges and opportunities that arise each year, this group plays a crucial part in the success of Coffee House's mission.

Recent Publisher's Circle members include many anonymous donors, Suzanne Allen, Patricia A. Beithon, the E. Thomas Binger & Rebecca Rand Fund of the Minneapolis Foundation, Andrew Brantingham, Robert & Gail Buuck, Claire Casey, Louise Copeland, Jane Dalrymple-Hollo, Mary Ebert & Paul Stembler, Kaywin Feldman & Jim Lutz, Chris Fischbach & Katie Dublinski, Sally French, Jocelyn Hale & Glenn Miller, the Rehael Fund-Roger Hale/Nor Hall of the Minneapolis Foundation, Randy Hartten & Ron Lotz, Dylan Hicks & Nina Hale, William Hardacker, Randall Heath, Jeffrey Hom, Carl & Heidi Horsch, Amy L. Hubbard & Geoffrey J. Kehoe Fund, Kenneth Kahn & Susan Dicker, Stephen & Isabel Keating, Kenneth Koch Literary Estate, Cinda Kornblum, Jennifer Kwon Dobbs & Stefan Liess, Lambert Family Foundation, Lenfestey Family Foundation, Sarah Lutman & Rob Rudolph, the Carol & Aaron Mack Charitable Fund of the Minneapolis Foundation, George & Olga Mack, Joshua Mack & Ron Warren, Gillian McCain, Malcolm S. McDermid & Katie Windle, Mary & Malcolm McDermid, Sjur Midness & Briar Andresen, Maureen Millea Smith & Daniel Smith, Peter Nelson & Jennifer Swenson, Enrique & Jennifer Olivarez, Alan Polsky, Marc Porter & James Hennessy, Robin Preble, Alexis Scott, Ruth Stricker Dayton, Jeffrey Sugerman & Sarah Schultz, Nan G. & Stephen C. Swid, Kenneth Thorp in memory of Allan Kornblum & Rochelle Ratner, Patricia Tilton, Joanne Von Blon, Stu Wilson & Melissa Barker, Warren D. Woessner & Iris C. Freeman, Margaret Wurtele, and Wayne P. Zink & Christopher Schout.

For more information about the Publisher's Circle and other ways to support Coffee House Press books, authors, and activities, please visit www.coffeehousepress.org/support or contact us at info@coffeehousepress.org.

ASHLEY TOLIVER is the author of the chapbook *Ideal Machine* (Poor Claudia 2014). A recipient of fellowships from the Cave Canem Foundation and Brown University, Ashley has had poems appear in *Third Coast, BOMB, Quarterly West, Copper Nickel, Design Observer,* and more. Born in San Francisco, she now lives in Portland, Oregon.

Spectra was designed by
Bookmobile Design & Digital Publisher Services.
Text is set in Adobe Garamond Pro.